THE BROCKHAMPTON LIBRARY

book

Gir es

BROCKHAMPTON PRESS
LONDON

This edition published 1996 by Brockhampton Press,
a member of Hodder Headline PLC Group.

ISBN 1 86019 213 0

Printed and bound in the UK

Abbie, Abby diminutive forms of **Abigail**, also used independently.

Aberah a variant form of **Averah**.

Abigail my father's joy (*Hebrew*); diminutive forms are **Abbie, Abby, Gail**.

Abra mother of multitudes (*Hebrew*).

Acacia the name of a plant, possibly meaning immortality and resurrection, used as a first name (*Greek*).

Acantha thorny, spiney (*Greek*).

Ada diminutive of **Adela** or names beginning with *Ada-*, also used independently; a variant form of **Adah**.

Adabelle joyful and beautiful, a combination of **Ada** and **Belle**; variant forms are **Adabel, Adabela, Adabella**.

Adah ornament (*Hebrew*); a variant form is **Ada**.

Adalia an early Saxon tribal name whose origin is unknown (*Germanic*).

Adar fire; as the name in the Jewish calendar for the twelfth month of the Biblical year and the sixth month of the civil year, it is a name sometimes given to girls born in that period (*Hebrew*).

Addie diminutive of **Adelaide**.

Adela of noble birth; a princess (*Germanic*).

Adelaide of noble birth; a princess (*Germanic*); a diminutive form is **Addie**.

Adèle, Adele the French form of **Adela**, now also used as an English form.

Adelheid noble kind (*Germanic*); a diminutive form is **Heidi**.

Adeline, Adelina of noble birth; a princess (*Germanic*); a diminutive form is **Aline**.

Adelphia sisterly, eternal

friend of mankind (*Greek*); variant forms are **Adelfia, Adelpha**.

Adina voluptuous, ripe, mature (*Hebrew*).

Adolpha noble she-wolf, she who will give her life for her young, the feminine form of Adolf (*Germanic*); variant forms are **Adolfa, Adolfina, Adolphina**.

Adonia beautiful goddess of the resurrection; eternal renewal of youth (*Greek*).

Adora adored and beloved gift (*Latin*).

Adorabella beautiful gift, a combination of **Adora** and **Bella**.

Adorna adorned with jewels (*Latin*).

Adrianne, Adrienne feminine forms of Adrian.

Aefa a variant form of **Aoife**.

Afra a variant form of **Aphra**.

Africa the name of the continent used as a first name.

Agatha good; kind (*Greek*); a diminutive form is **Aggie, Aggy**.

Agave illustrious, famous (*Greek*).

Aggie, Aggy diminutive forms of **Agatha, Agnes**.

Agnes chaste; pure (*Greek*); diminutive forms are **Aggie, Aggy, Agneta, Nessa, Nessie**.

Agnès the French form of **Agnes**.

Agnese the Italian form of **Agnes**.

Ailean Scots Gaelic form of **Alan**.

Aileen a variant form of **Eileen**.

Ailsa fairy (*Scots Gaelic*).

Aimée the French form of **Amy**.

Áine an Irish Gaelic form of **Anna**.

Aisleen, Aisling vision (*Irish Gaelic*).

Alana, Alanna, Alannah feminine forms of Alan; a variant form is **Lana**.

Alarice ruler (*Germanic*); variant forms are **Alarica, Alarise**.

Alberta feminine form of Albert.

Albina white, very fair (*Latin*); variant forms are **Albinia, Alvina, Aubina, Aubine**.

Alcina strong-minded one, from a legendary woman who could make gold from stardust (*Greek*).

Alcyone in Greek mythology a woman who drowned herself from grief at her husband's death and who was turned into a kingfisher; variant forms are **Halcyone, Halcyon**.

Alda wise and rich (*Germanic*); variant forms are **Eada, Elda**.

Aldora of noble rank (*Old English*); variant forms are **Aelda, Aeldra**.

Aleria like an eagle (*Latin*).

Alethea truth (*Greek*).

Alexa diminutive of **Alexandra**.

Alexandra, Alexandrina feminine forms of Alexander; diminutive forms are **Alex, Alexa, Lexie, Lexy, Sandie, Sandra, Sandy**.

Alexia feminine form of Alexis.

Alexina feminine form of Alexander.

Alfonsine noble (*Germanic*); variant forms are **Alphonsina, Alphonsine, Alphonza**.

Alfreda feminine form of Alfred; diminutive forms are **Alfie, Allie**; variant forms are **Elfreda, Elfreida, Elfrieda, Elfrida, Elva, Elga, Freda**.

Alice, Alicia of noble birth; a princess (*Germanic*); variant forms are **Alys, Alyssa**.

Alida little bird; small and lithe (*Latin*); a Hungarian form of **Adelaide**; variant forms are **Aleda, Aleta, Alita**; diminutive forms are **Leda, Lita**.

Aliénor a French form of **Eleanor**.

Alima learned in music and dancing (*Arabic*).

Aline a contraction of **Adeline**.

Alison diminutive of **Alice**, now used entirely in its own right; a variant form is **Allison**; diminutive forms are **Allie, Ally**.

Alix a variant form of **Alex**.

Allegra a word for cheerful or blithe used as a first name (*Italian*).

Allie, Ally diminutive of **Alice, Alison**.

Allison a variant form of **Alison**.

Alma loving, nurturing (*Latin*).

Almira lofty; a princess (*Arabic*).

Aloha a word for welcome used as a first name (*Hawaiian*).

Alta tall in spirit (*Latin*).

Althea a healer (*Greek*); a diminutive form is **Thea**.

Alula winged one (*Latin*).

Alura divine counsellor (*Old English*).

Alva white (*Latin*).

Alvina, Alvine beloved and noble friend (*Germanic*); a diminutive form is **Vina**.

Alys, Alyssa variant forms of **Alice, Alicia**.

Alyth a placename, meaning steep place, used as a first name.

Alzena woman, purveyor of charm and virtue (*Arabic*).

Amabel lovable (*Latin*); a diminutive form is **Mabel**.

Amadea feminine form of Amadeus.

Amalia work (*Germanic*); an Italian and Greek form of **Amelia**.

Amanda worthy of love (*Latin*); diminutive forms are **Manda, Mandy**.

Amber the name of a gemstone used as a first name.

Ambrosine feminine form of Ambrose; variant forms are **Ambrosia, Ambrosina**.

Amelia busy, energetic (*Germanic*); a diminutive form is **Millie**.

Amélie the French form of **Amelia**.

Amelinda beloved and pretty (*Spanish*); variant forms are **Amalinda, Amelinde**.

Amena honest, truthful (*Gaelic*).

Amethyst the name of the semi-precious gemstone used as a first name (*Greek*).

Aminta, Amintha, Aminthe protector, a shepherdess in Greek mythology (*Greek*).

Amy beloved (*Old French*).

Anastasia rising up, resurrection (*Greek*); diminutive forms are **Stacey, Stacy, Stacie, Stasia**.

Anatholia, Anatola feminine forms of Anatole (*Greek*); a variant form is **Anatolia**.

Anatolia a variant form of **Anatholia**.

Andrea feminine form of

Andreas or Andrew; a variant form is **Andrina**.

Andrina, Andrine variant forms of **Andrea**.

Anemone windflower, the name of the garden plant used as a first name (*Greek*).

Angel diminutive of **Angela** (*Greek*).

Angela, Angelina messenger (*Greek*); diminutive forms are **Angel** and **Angie**.

Angelica lovely; angelic (*Greek*).

Angie a diminutive form of **Angela**.

Angharad much loved (*Welsh*).

Anita Spanish diminutive of **Ann**, now used independently as an English-language form; a diminutive form is **Nita**.

Ann grace (*Hebrew*); a variant form is **Hannah**; a diminutive form is **Annie**.

Anna the Latin form of **Ann**.

Annabel, Annabelle, Annabella lovable (possibly from **Amabel**); diminutive forms are **Bella, Belle**.

Anne the French form of **Ann**.

Anneka a Dutch diminutive of **Anna**.

Annette a French diminutive of **Ann**, used as an English-language form.

Annika a Swedish diminutive of **Anna**.

Annis, Annice a medieval diminutive of **Agnes**.

Annona a variant form of **Anona**.

Annunciata Italian form of *nuntius*, bringer of news, i.e. the angel Gabriel, who delivered the announcement of the Virgin Mary's conception, a name often given to children born on 25 March, Lady Day (*Latin*).

Anona annual crops, hence the Roman goddess of crops (*Latin*); a variant form is **Annona**; diminutives are **Nonnie, Nona**.

Anora light, graceful (*Old English*).

Anselma feminine form of Anselm; a variant form is **Arselma**.

Anthea flowery (*Greek*).

Antoinette a diminutive form of **Antonia**, now commonly used as an English-language form; a diminutive form is **Toinette**.

Antonia feminine form of Antony; diminutive forms are **Toni, Tonia, Tonie, Tony**.

Anwen very beautiful (*Welsh*).

Aoife the Irish Gaelic form of **Eve**; a variant form is **Aefa**.

Aphra dust (*Hebrew*); woman from Carthage (*Latin*); a variant form is **Afra**.

April the name of the month, *Aprilis*, used as a personal name (*Latin*).

Ara spirit of revenge, and the goddess of destruction and vengeance (*Greek*).

Arabella, Arabela a fair altar (*Latin*); a woman (*Arabic*); diminutive forms are **Bella, Belle**.

Araminta beautiful, sweet-smelling flower (*Greek*); a diminutive form is **Minta**.

Ardath field of flowers (*Hebrew*); variant forms are **Aridatha, Ardatha**.

Ardella, Ardelle, Ardelis enthusiasm, warmth (*Hebrew*).

Areta, Aretha excellently virtuous (*Greek*); variant forms are **Aretta, Arette, Aretas**.

Aretta, Arette variant forms of **Areta**.

Argenta, Argente, Argente silver or silvery coloured (*Latin*).

Aria the Italian word for beautiful melody, from *aer*, 'breeze' (*Latin*), used as a first name.

Ariadne very holy (*Greek*).

Arianna an Italian form of **Ariadne**.

Arianne a French form of **Ariadne**.

Ariella, Arielle feminine forms of Ariel (*Hebrew*).

Arlene form of **Arlen**; a variant form of **Charlene, Marlene**; variant forms are **Arleen, Arlena, Arlina, Arline, Arlyne**.

Armilla bracelet (*Latin*).

Armina, Armine feminine forms of Armin; variant forms are **Erminie, Erminia**.

Arselma a variant form of **Anselma**.

Artemis the name of the virgin Greek goddess of hunting

and the moon, the derivation of which is unknown. The Roman equivalent is Diana.

Arva ploughed land, pasture (*Latin*).

Arwenna feminine form of Arwyn.

Asphodel a daffodil-like plant, the origin of whose name is obscure, used as a first name (*Greek*).

Astra diminutive of **Astrid**.

Astrid fair god (*Norse*); a diminutive is **Astra**.

Atalanta, Atalante the name of a mythological character who agreed to marry the man who could outrun her (*Greek*); a variant form is **Atlanta**.

Atalya guardian (*Spanish*).

Athena, Ahthene, Atheneé in Greek mythology, the goddess of wisdom. Her Roman counterpart is Minerva (*Greek*).

Atlante a variant form of **Atalanta**.

Audrey noble might (*Old English*).

Augusta feminine form of Augustus; diminutive forms are **Gussie, Gusta**.

Aura, Aure, Aurea breath of air (*Latin*); a variant form is **Auria**.

Aurelia feminine form of Aurelius.

Aurelié the French form of **Aurelia**.

Auria a variant form of **Aura**.

Aurora morning redness; fresh; brilliant (*Latin*).

Autumn the name of the season, the origin of which is uncertain, used as a first name.

Ava origin uncertain, perhaps a Germanic diminutive of names beginning *Av-*.

Avera transgressor (*Hebrew*); a variant form is **Aberah**.

Averil, Averill English forms of **Avril**.

Avice, Avis possibly bird (*Latin*).

Avril the French form of **April**.

Ayesha the name of the favourite wife of the Prophet Mohammad.

Azaliea, Azalia, Azalee variant forms of the name of the azalea plant, supposed to prefer dry earth, used as a first name.

Azura, Azure blue as the sky (*French*).

Bab, Babs diminutive forms of **Barbara**.

Bambi a variant form of the word for *bambino*, child (*Italian*).

Baptista feminine form of Baptist.

Barbara, Barbra foreign, strange (*Greek*); diminutive forms are **Bab, Babs, Barbie**.

Basilia feminine form of Basil.

Bathilda battle commander (*Germanic*).

Bathilde the French form of **Bathilda**.

Bathsheba daughter of plenty (*Hebrew*).

Bea a diminutive form of **Beatrice, Beatrix**.

Beata blessed, divine one (*Latin*); a diminutive form is **Bea**.

Beatrice, Beatrix woman who blesses (*Latin*); diminutive forms are **Bea, Beatie, Beaty, Bee, Trix, Trixie**.

Beckie, Becky diminutive forms of **Rebecca**.

Beda maid of war (*Old English*).

Bee a diminutive form of **Beatrice**.

Belinda a name used by Sir John Vanburgh in his play *The Provok'd Wife*, its origin is uncertain, possibly beautiful woman (*Italian*).

Bella, Belle beautiful (*French, Italian*); diminutive forms of **Annabel, Arabella, Isabella**.

Bena wise one (*Hebrew*).

Benedicta feminine form of Benedict; a contracted form is **Benita**; a diminutive form is **Dixie**.

Benita a contracted form of **Benedicta**.

Berenice bringing victory (*Greek*); *also* **Bernice**.

Bernadette feminine form of Bernard.

Bernice a variant form of **Berenice**.

Berta a German, Italian and Spanish form of **Bertha**.

Bertha bright; beautiful; famous (*Germanic*); a diminutive form is **Bertie**.

Beryl jewel (*Greek*), the name of the gemstone used as a first name.

Bess, Bessie diminutive forms of **Elizabeth**.

Beth a diminutive form of **Elizabeth, Bethany,** now used independently.

Bethan a Welsh diminutive form of **Elizabeth-Ann** also used independently.

Bethany a placename near Jerusalem, the home of Lazarus in the New Testament and meaning house of poverty, used as a first name (*Aramaic*).

Betsy, Bette, Bettina, Betty diminutive forms of **Eliza-beth**.

Beulah married (*Hebrew*).

Bianca the Italian form of **Blanch**, now also used independently as an English-language form.

Biddy a diminutive form of **Bridget**.

Bina, Binah, Bine bee (*Hebrew*).

Binnie a diminutive form of **Sabina**.

Birgit the Swedish form of **Bridget**; a diminutive form is **Britt**.

Blanche white (*Germanic*).

Blodwen white flower (*Welsh*).

Blossom like a flower (*Old English*).

Bonita pretty (*Spanish*); good (*Latin*); a diminutive form is **Bonnie**.

Bonnie pretty (*Scots English*); a diminutive form of **Bonita**.

Branwen raven-haired beauty (*Welsh*); a variant form of **Bronwen**.

Brenda a brand or sword (*Old Norse*).

Brenna raven-haired beauty (*Irish Gaelic*).

Bridget strong (*Celtic*); a variant form is **Brigid**; diminutive forms are **Biddy, Bridie**.

Brigid a variant form of **Bridget**.

Brigitte a French form of **Bridget**.

Briony a variant form of **Bryony**.

Britt a diminutive form of **Birgit**, used independently.

Bronwen white breast (*Welsh*); variant forms are **Bronwyn, Branwen**.

Brook, Brooke a surname, meaning stream, used as a first name; a variant form is **Brooks**.

Brunhilda, Brunhilde warrior maid (*Germanic*).

Bryony the name of a climbing plant used as a first name (*Greek*); a variant form is **Briony**.

Bunty a diminutive meaning lamb, now used as a first name (*English*).

Caddie a diminutive form of **Carol, Carola, Carole, Caroline, Carolyn**.

Cadence rhythmic (*Latin*).

Cadenza the Italian form of **Cadence**.

Cáit the Irish Gaelic form of **Kate**.

Caitlín, Caitrín Irish Gaelic forms of **Katherine**.

Cal a diminutive form of **Calandra, Calantha**.

Calandra from the Greek meaning a lark; diminutive forms are **Cal, Callie, Cally**.

Calantha beautiful blossom (*Greek*); diminutive forms are **Cal, Callie, Cally**.

Caledonia the Roman name for Scotland used as a first name (*Latin*).

Calla beautiful (*Greek*).

Callie a diminutive form of **Calandra, Calantha**.

Calliope lovely voice; the muse of poetry (*Greek*).

Cally a diminutive form of **Calandra, Calantha**.

Calypso concealer; in Greek mythology, the sea nymph who held Odysseus captive for seven years (*Greek*); a variant form is **Kalypso**.

Camilla votaress, attendant at a sacrifice (*Latin*).

Camille the French form of **Camilla**.

Candice, Candace meaning uncertain, possibly brilliantly white or pure and virtuous, the name of an Ethiopian queen (*Latin*); diminutive forms are **Candie, Candy**.

Candida shining white (*Latin*); diminutive forms are **Candie, Candy**.

Candie a diminutive form of **Candice, Candida**.

Candy a diminutive form of **Candice, Candida**; a name used in its own right, from candy, the American-English word for a sweet.

Cara friend (*Irish Gaelic*); dear, darling (*Italian*); a variant form is **Carina**.

Caridad the Spanish form of **Charity**.

Carina a variant form of **Cara**.

Carissa dear one (*Latin*).

Carla form of **Carl**; a variant form is **Carlin**; diminutive forms are **Carlie, Carley, Carly**.

Carlie a diminutive form of **Carla, Carlin**.

Carlin a variant form of **Carla**; diminutive forms are **Carlie, Carley, Carly**.

Carlotta the Italian form of **Charlotte**.

Carly a diminutive form of **Carla, Carlin**, now used independently.

Carmel garden (*Hebrew*).

Carmela a Spanish and the Italian forms of **Carmel**.

Carmen a Spanish form of **Carmel**.

Carnation the name of a flower, meaning flesh colour, sometimes used as a first name (*Latin/French*).

Carola a variant form of **Caroline**; diminutive forms are **Carrie, Caro, Caddie**.

Carole the French form of **Carol**; a contracted form of **Caroline**; diminutive forms are **Caro, Carrie, Caddie**.

Carolina the Italian and Spanish forms of **Caroline**.

Caroline, Carolyn womanly (Latin); diminutive forms are **Caro, Carrie, Caddie**.

Carrie a diminutive form of

Carol, Carola, Carole, Caroline, Carolyn.
Carys love (*Welsh*).
Cass a diminutive form of **Cassandra**.
Cassandra she who inflames with love (*Greek*); in Greek mythology, a princess whose prophecies of doom were not believed; diminutive forms are **Cass, Cassie**.
Cassie a diminutive form of **Cassandra**.
Catalina the Spanish form of **Katherine**.
Caterina the Italian form of **Katherine**.
Catharina, Catharine, Catherina variant forms of **Catherine**.
Catherine the French form of **Katherine**, now used as an English-language form; diminutive forms are **Cath, Cathie, Cathy**.
Catrin the Welsh form of **Katherine**.
Catriona the Scots Gaelic form of **Katherine**.
Cecile the French form of **Cecily, Cecilia**.
Cecily, Cecilia feminine forms of Cecil; diminutive forms are **Celia, Cis, Cissie, Cissy**; a variant form is **Cicely**.
Celandine the name of either of two unrelated flowering plants, meaning swallow, used as a first name (*Greek*).
Celeste, **Celestine** heavenly (*Latin*).
Celia heavenly (*Latin*); diminutive form of **Cecilia**.
Cendrillon from the ashes, the fairytale heroine (*French*); the anglicized form is **Cinderella**.
Cerian diminutive form of **Ceri**.
Cerys love (*Welsh*).
Chandra moon brighter than the stars (*Sanskrit*).
Chanel the surname of the French couturier and perfumier, Coco Chanel, used as a first name.
Charis grace (*Greek*).
Charity the abstract noun for the quality of tolerance or generosity used as a personal name (*Old French*).
Charlene a relatively modern diminutive feminized form of Charles.

Charley diminutive form of **Charlotte**.

Charlotte feminine form of Charles (*Germanic*); diminutive forms are **Charlie, Charley, Lottie**.

Charmaine a diminutive form of the abstract noun for the quality of pleasing or attracting people used as a first name; a variant form of **Charmian**.

Charmian little delight (*Greek*); a modern variant form is **Charmaine**.

Chelsea a placename, meaning chalk landing place, sometimes used as a first name (*Old English*).

Cher, Chérie dear, darling (*French*).

Cherry the name of the fruit used as a first name; a form of **Chérie**; a variant form is **Cheryl**.

Cheryl a variant form of **Cherry**; a combining form of **Cherry** and **Beryl**; a variant form is **Sheryl**.

Chiara the Italian form of **Clara**.

Chiquita little one (*Spanish*).

Chloë, Chloe a green herb; a young shoot (*Greek*).

Chloris green (*Greek*).

Chrissie a diminutive form of **Christiana, Christine**.

Christabel a combination of **Christine** and **Bella** coined by Samuel Taylor Coleridge for a poem of this name.

Christian belonging to Christ; a believer in Christ (*Latin*); diminutive forms are **Chris, Christie, Christy**.

Christiana feminine form of Christian; a variant form is **Christina**.

Christina a variant form of **Christiana**.

Christine a French form of **Christina**, used as an English-language form; diminutive forms are **Chris, Chrissie, Christie, Christy, Tina**.

Christy a variant form of **Christie**.

Chrystal a variant form of **Crystal**.

Ciara feminine form of Ciarán.

Cicely a variant form of **Cecilia**.

Cilla a diminutive form of **Priscilla** (*French*).

Cinderella the anglicized form of **Cendrillon**, the fairytale heroine; diminutive forms are **Cindie, Cindy, Ella**.

Cindy a diminutive form of **Cinderella, Cynthia, Lucinda**, now often used independently.

Cinzia the Italian form of **Cynthia**.

Claire the French form of **Clara**, now used widely as an English form.

Clara bright, illustrious, renowned (*Latin*); a variant form is **Clare**; a diminutive form is **Clarrie**.

Clarabel, Clarabella, Clarabelle a combination of **Clara** and **Bella** or **Belle**, meaning bright, shining beauty (*Latin/French*); a variant form is **Claribel**.

Clare a variant form of **Clara**; a surname, meaning bright or shining, used as a first name (*Latin*).

Claribel a variant form of **Clarabel**.

Clarice fame (*Latin*); a variant form of **Clara**; a variant form is **Clarissa**.

Clarinda a combination of **Clara** and **Belinda** or **Lucinda**.

Clarissa a variant form of **Clarice**.

Clarrie a diminutive form of **Clara**.

Claudia feminine form of Claud.

Clem a diminutive form of **Clematis, Clemency, Clementine, Clementina**.

Clematis climbing plant (*Greek*), the name of a climbing plant with white, blue or purple flowers used as a first name; diminutive forms are **Clem, Clemmie**.

Clemency the abstract noun for the quality of tempering justice with mercy, used as a first name (*Latin*); a variant form is **Clemence**; diminutive forms are **Clem, Clemmie**.

Clementine, Clementina feminine forms of Clement; diminutive forms are **Clem, Clemmie**.

Cleo a short form of **Cleopatra**, used independently.

Cleopatra father's glory (*Greek*); a diminutive form is **Cleo**.

Cliantha glory flower (*Greek*); a diminutive form is **Clia**.
Clio glory (*Greek*).
Clorinda a combination of **Chloris** and **Belinda** or **Lucinda**.
Clothilde, Clotilde famous fighting woman (*Germanic*).
Clover the name of a flowering plant used as a first name (*English*).
Colette a diminutive form of **Nicole**, now used independently; a variant form is **Collette**.
Colleen the Irish word for a girl, used as a first name.
Collette a variant form of **Colette**.
Columbine little dove; the name of a flowering plant, used as a first name (*Latin*).
Comfort the abstract noun for the state of well-being or the bringer of solace, and used as a first name in the Puritan tradition (*Latin/French*).
Concepcion beginning, a reference to the Immaculate Conception of the Virgin Mary (*Spanish*); diminutive forms are **Concha, Conchita**.
Concepta the Latin form of **Concetta**.
Concetta conceptive, a reference to the Virgin Mary and the Immaculate Conception (*Italian*).
Concha, Conchita diminutive forms of **Concepcion**.
Consolata consoling, a reference to the Virgin Mary (*Italian*).
Consolation the abstract noun for the act of consoling or the state of solace; used as a first name in the Puritan tradition.
Constance feminine form of Constant; diminutive forms are **Con, Connie**; a variant form is **Constanta**.
Consuela consolation, a reference to the Virgin Mary (*Spanish*).
Cora maiden (*Greek*).
Corabella, Corabelle beautiful maiden, a combination of **Cora** and **Bella**.
Coral the name of the pink marine jewel material used as a first name.
Coralie the French form of **Coral**.
Cordelia warm-hearted (*Latin*).

Corinna, Corinne variant forms of **Cora**.

Cornelia feminine form of Cornelius.

Corona crown (*Latin*).

Cosima feminine form of Cosmo.

Courtney a surname, meaning short nose, used as a first name; also used as a boy's name (*Old French*).

Cressida gold (*Greek*); a contracted form is **Cressa**.

Cristal a variant form of **Crystal**.

Cristina the Italian, Portuguese and Spanish form of **Christina**.

Crystal the name of a very clear brilliant glass used as a first name; variant forms are **Cristal, Chrystal**.

Cynthia belonging to Mount Cynthus (*Greek*); diminutive forms are **Cindie, Cindy**.

Cyrene, Cyrena from Cyrene, an ancient city of North Africa; in mythology, a water nymph loved by Apollo (*Greek*); a variant form is **Kyrena**.

Cytherea from Cythera, an island off the southern coast of the Peloponnese; in Greek mythology, home of a cult of Aphrodite the Greek goddess of love (*Greek*).

Cythereia from Cytherea, in Greek mythology, an alternative name for Aphrodite the Greek goddess of love.

Daffodil the name of the spring plant that yields bright yellow flowers used as a first name (*Dutch/Latin*); a diminutive form is **Daffy**.

Dagmar bright day (*Norse*).

Dahlia the name of the plant with brightly coloured flowers, named after the Swedish botanist Anders Dahl (dale), used as a first name.

Daisy the name of the plant; the day's eye (*Old English*).

Daley a surname, meaning assembly, used as a first name (*Irish Gaelic*); a variant form is **Daly**.

Dalilah, Dalila variant forms of **Delilah**.

Daly a variant of **Daley**.

Dana a surname, of uncertain meaning, possibly meaning from Denmark, sometimes used as a first name (*Old English*).

Danaë in Greek mythology, the mother of Perseus by Zeus, who came to her as a shower of gold while she was in prison; diminutive forms are **Dannie, Danny**.

Danielle feminine form of Daniel.

Daphne laurel (*Greek*).

Dara charity (*Hebrew*).

Darcie feminine form of Darcy.

Daria a feminine form of Darius.

Darlene, Darleen the endearment 'darling' combined with a suffix to form a first name (*Old English*).

Darrelle feminine form of Darrell (*French*).

Darryl a variant form of **Darrelle**, also used as a boy's name.

Daryl a variant form of **Darrelle**, also used as a boy's name.

Davina feminine form of David.

Dawn the name of the first part of the day derived from the Latin *Aurora* and used as a personal name in the English form.

Deana, Deane feminine forms of Dean; variant forms are **Dena, Dene**.

Deanna a variant form of **Diana**.

Deborah, Debra bee (*Hebrew*); diminutive forms are **Deb, Debbie, Debby**.

Decima feminine form of Decimus.

Dee a diminutive form of names beginning with *D*.

Deirdre meaning uncertain, possibly sorrowful (*Irish Gaelic*).

Delfine a variant form of **Delphine**.

Delia woman of Delos (*Greek*).

Delicia great delight (*Latin*).

Delight the abstract noun for great pleasure, satisfaction or joy used as a first name (*Old French*).

Delilah, Delila meaning uncertain, possibly delicate (*Hebrew*); variant forms are **Dalila, Dalilah**; a diminutive form is **Lila**.

Delma feminine form of Delmar; a diminutive form of **Fidelma**.

Delores a variant form of **Dolores**.

Delphine dolphin *(Latin)*; a variant form is **Delfine**.

Delyth pretty (*Welsh*).

Dena, Dene variant forms of **Deana**.

Denice a variant form of **Denise**.

Denise feminine form of Denis; a variant form is **Denice**.

Desdemona ill-fated (*Greek*), the name given by Shakespeare to the wife of Othello.

Desirée longed for (*French*).

Di a diminutive form of **Diana, Diane, Dianne, Dina, Dinah**.

Diana goddess (*Latin*); a diminutive form is **Di**.

Diane, Dianne French forms of **Diana**.

Dido teacher (*Greek*), in Greek mythology a princess from Tyre who founded Carthage and became its queen.

Dilys sure, genuine (*Welsh*); a diminutive form is **Dilly**.

Dina feminine form of Dino; a variant form of **Dinah**.

Dinah vindicated (*Hebrew*); a variant form is **Dina**; a diminutive form is **Di**.

Dione, Dionne daughter of heaven and earth (*Greek*), in Greek mythology the earliest consort of Zeus and mother of Aphrodite.

Dixie a diminutive form of Benedicta.

Dodie, Dodo diminutive forms of **Dorothy**.

Dolina a Scottish variant form of **Donalda**.

Dolly a diminutive form of **Dorothy**.

Dolores sorrows (*Spanish*); a variant form is **Delores**; diminutive forms are **Lola, Lolita**.

Donalda feminine form of Donald.

Donna lady (*Italian*).

Dora a diminutive form of **Dorothea, Theodora**, etc., now used independently; diminutive forms are **Dorrie, Dorry**.

Dorcas a gazelle (*Greek*).

Doreen an Irish variant form of **Dora**.

Dorinda lovely gift (*Greek*); diminutive forms are **Dorrie, Dorry**.

Doris Dorian woman, one of a Hellenic people who invaded Greece in the 2nd century BC (*Greek*); diminutive forms are **Dorrie, Dorry**.

Dorothea a German form of **Dorothy**; a diminutive form is **Thea**.

Dorothée a French form of **Dorothea**.

Dorothy the gift of God (*Greek*); diminutive forms are **Dodie, Dodo, Dolly, Dot**.

Dorrie, Dorry diminutive forms of **Dora, Dorinda, Doris**.

Drusilla with dewy eyes (*Latin*).

Dulcie a diminutive form of **Dulcibella**. meaning sweet beautiful (*Latin*).

Dyan, Dyane a variant form of **Diane**.

Dymphna little fawn (*Irish Gaelic*).

Éanna bird (*Irish Gaelic*); an anglicized form is **Enda**.

Earlene, Earline feminine forms of Earl; variant forms are **Erlene, Erline**; diminutive forms are **Earlie, Earley**.

Eartha of the earth (*Old English*); a variant form is **Ertha**.

Easter the name of the

Christian festival, used as a first name.

Ebba wild boar (*Germanic*); an old form of **Eve**.

Ebony the name of the dark, hard wood used as a first name.

Echo the name for the physical phenomenon of the reflection of sound or other radiation, used as a first name; in Greek mythology it is the name of the nymph who pined away for love of Narcissus.

Eda prosperity, happiness (*Old English*).

Edana feminine form of Edan.

Edie a diminutive form of **Edina, Edith, Edwina**.

Edina a Scottish variant form of **Edwina**.

Edith prosperity strife (*Old English*); variant forms are **Edyth, Edythe**; diminutive forms are **Edie, Edy**.

Edlyn noble maid (*Old English*).

Edmonda feminine form of Edmund (*Old English*).

Edna pleasure (*Hebrew*).

Edwardina feminine form of Edward.

Edwina feminine form of Edwin; a variant form is **Edina**.

Edy a diminutive form of **Edith**.

Edyth, Edythe variant forms of **Edith**.

Effie a diminutive form of **Euphemia**.

Eglantine an alternative name for the wild rose, meaning sharp, keen, used as a first name (*Old French*).

Eileen the Irish form of **Helen**; a variant form is **Aileen**.

Eilidh a Scots Gaelic form of **Helen**.

Eira snow (*Welsh*).

Eirlys snowdrop (*Welsh*).

Eithne kernel (*Irish Gaelic*); anglicized forms are **Ena, Ethna**.

Elaine a French form of **Helen**.

Eldora a shortened form of *El Dorado*, meaning the land of gold, used as a first name (*Spanish*).

Eldrida feminine form of Eldrid.

Eleanor, Eleanore medieval French variant forms of

Helen; a variant form is **Elinor**; diminutive forms are **Ella, Nell, Nora**.

Eleanora the Italian form of **Eleanor**.

Electra brilliant (*Greek*).

Elen angel, nymph (*Welsh*).

Elena the Italian and Spanish form of **Helen**.

Eleonora the Italian form of **Eleanor**.

Eleonore the German form of **Eleanor**.

Eléonore a French form of **Leonora**.

Elfleda noble beauty (*Old English*).

Elfreda elf strength (*Old English*).

Elga holy (*Old Norse*); a variant form of **Olga**.

Elin a Welsh diminutive form of **Elinor**; a Welsh variant form of **Helen**.

Elinor a variant form of **Eleanor**.

Elisa an Italian diminutive form of **Elisabetta**.

Elisabeth a French and German form of **Elizabeth**.

Elisabetta an Italian form of **Elizabeth**.

Élise a French diminutive form of **Elisabeth**.

Elizabeth worshipper of God; consecrated to God (*Hebrew*); diminutive forms are **Bess, Bet, Beth, Betsy, Betty, Eliza, Elsa, Elsie, Libby, Lisa, Liza, Lisbeth, Liz**.

Ella a diminutive form of **Cinderella, Eleanor, Isabella**.

Ellen a variant form of **Helen**.

Ellice the feminine form of **Elias, Ellis**.

Ellie a diminutive form of **Alice**.

Elma a diminutive form of **Wilhelmina**; a contracted form of **Elizabeth Mary**.

Éloise, Eloisa sound, whole (*Germanic*); a variant form is **Héloïse**.

Elsa a diminutive form of **Alison, Alice, Elizabeth**.

Elsie a diminutive form of **Alice, Alison, Elizabeth, Elspeth**.

Elspeth, Elspet Scottish forms of **Elizabeth**; diminutive forms are **Elsie, Elspie**.

Eluned idol (*Welsh*).

Elva elf friend (*Old English*); a variant form is **Elvina**.

Elvina a variant form of **Elva**.

Elvira white (*Latin*).

Emeline a variant form of **Amelia**; a diminutive form of **Emma**; a variant form is **Emmeline**.

Emerald the name of the green gemstone used as a first name.

Emilia the Italian form of **Emily**.

Emilie the German form of **Emily**.

Émilie the French form of **Emily**.

Emily of a noble Roman family the origin of whose name, *Aemilius*, is uncertain.

Emma whole, universal (*Germanic*); diminutive forms are **Emm, Emmie**.

Emmeline a variant form of **Emeline**.

Ena an anglicized form of **Eithne**.

Enda an anglicized form of **Éanna**.

Enfys rainbow (*Welsh*).

Enid meaning uncertain, possibly woodlark (*Welsh*).

Enrica the Italian form of **Henrietta**.

Enrichetta the Italian form of **Henrietta**.

Enriqueta the Spanish form of **Henrietta**.

Eranthe flower of spring (*Greek*).

Erda of the earth (*Germanic*).

Erica feminine form of Eric; a variant form is **Erika**.

Erika a variant form of **Erica**.

Erin the poetic name for Ireland, used as a first name.

Erlene, Erline variant forms of **Earlene, Erline**; diminutive forms are **Erlie, Erley**.

Erma warrior maid (*Germanic*).

Erna a diminutive form of **Ernesta, Ernestine**.

Ernesta feminine form of Ernest; a diminutive form is **Erna**.

Ernestine feminine form of Ernest; diminutive forms are **Erna, Tina**.

Esmé beloved (*French*).

Esmeralda a Spanish form of **Emerald**.

Esta a variant form of **Esther**.

Estelle, Estella variant forms of **Stella**.

Ester the Italian and Spanish forms of **Esther**.

Esther the planet Venus (*Persian*); a variant form is **Esta**; diminutive forms are **Ess, Essie, Tess, Tessie**.

Estrella the Spanish form of **Estelle**.

Ethel noble; of noble birth (*Old English*).

Ethna an anglicized form of **Eithne**.

Etta, Ettie diminutive forms of **Henrietta**.

Eudora good gift (*Greek*).

Eufemia the Italian and Spanish form of **Euphemia**.

Eugenia feminine form of **Eugene**; diminutive forms are **Ena, Gene**.

Eugénie the French form of **Eugenia**.

Eulalie fair speech (*Greek*).

Eunice good victory (*Greek*).

Euphemia of good report (*Greek*); diminutive forms are **Fay, Effie, Phamie, Phemie**.

Eustacia feminine form of Eustace; diminutive forms are **Stacey, Stacie, Stacy**.

Eva the German, Italian, and Spanish forms of **Eve**.

Evadne of uncertain meaning, possibly high-born (*Greek*).

Evangeline good tidings (*Greek*).

Eve life (*Hebrew*); diminutive forms are **Evie, Evelina, Eveline, Eveleen**.

Eveline a diminutive form of **Eva, Eve**.

Evelyn the English surname, used as a first name.

Evita Spanish diminutive form of **Eva**.

Evodia good journey (*Greek*).

Fabia a feminine form of Fabian; a variant form is **Fabiola**.

Fabienne feminine form of Fabien.

Fabiola a variant form of **Fabia**.

Faith the quality of belief or fidelity, used as a first name (*Old English*).

Fanchon a diminutive form of **Françoise**.

Fanny a diminutive form of **Frances**, also used independently.

Fatima the name of the daughter of Mohammed (*Semitic*); of Fatima in Portugal (*Portuguese*).

Faustina, Faustine lucky (*Latin*).

Favor, Favour an abstract noun, meaning good will or an act of good will, from *favere*, to protect, used as a first name (*Latin*).

Fawn the name for a young deer or a light greyish-brown colour used as a first name (*Old French*).

Fay, Faye faith or fairy (*Old French*); a diminutive form of **Euphemia**.

Felicia feminine form of Felix.

Felicidad the Spanish form of **Felicia**.

Felicie the Italian form of **Felicia**.

Felicity happiness (*Latin*).

Fenella an anglicized form of **Fionnuala**.

Fern the name of the plant sometimes used as a first name (*Old English*).

Fernanda feminine form of Ferdinand.

Ffion foxglove (*Welsh*).

Fid a diminutive form of **Fidelia, Fidelis**.

Fidelia a variant form of **Fidelis**; a diminutive form is **Fid**.

Fidelis faithful (*Latin*); a variant form is **Fidelia**; a diminutive form is **Fid**.

Fidelma faithful Mary (*Latin/ Irish Gaelic*); a diminutive form is **Delma**.

Fifi a French diminutive form of **Josephine**.

Filippa the Italian form of **Philippa**.

Finola a variant form of **Fionnuala**.

Fiona white, fair (*Scots Gaelic*).

Fionnuala white shoulder (*Irish Gaelic*); a diminutive form is **Nuala**, also used independently.

Flanna feminine form of Flann.

Flavia yellow-haired, golden (*Latin*).

Fleur a flower; the French form of Florence.

Fleurette little flower (*French*).

Flo a diminutive form of **Flora, Florence**.

Flora flowers; the Roman goddess of flowers (*Latin*); diminutive forms are **Flo, Florrie, Flossie**.

Florence blooming; flourishing (*Latin*); diminutive forms are **Flo, Florrie, Flossie, Floy**.

Florrie, Flossie diminutive forms of **Flora, Florence**.

Flower the English word for a bloom or blossom used as a first name.

Floy a diminutive form of **Flora, Florence**.

Fortune the word for wealth, fate or chance used as a first name (*Latin*); a variant form is **Fortuna**.

Fran a diminutive form of **Frances**.

Franca a diminutive form of **Francesca**.

Frances a feminine form of Francis; diminutive forms are **Fanny, Fran, Francie**.

Francesca the Italian form of **Frances**.

Francie a diminutive form of **Frances**.

Francine a diminutive form of **Frances, Françoise**.

Francisca the Spanish form of **Frances**.

Françoise the French form of **Frances**.

Freda a diminutive form of **Winifred**; a variant form of **Frieda**.

Frederica feminine form of Frederick; diminutive forms are **Fred, Freddie, Freddy, Frieda**.

Frédérique the French form of **Frederica**.

Freya lady, the Norse goddess of love (*Norse*).

Frieda peace (*Germanic*); a diminutive form of **Frederica**.

Friede the German form of **Frieda**.

Friederike the German form of **Frederica**; a diminutive form is **Fritzi**.

Fritzi a diminutive form of **Friederike**.

Fulvia yellow-haired (*Latin*).

Gabbie, Gabby diminutive forms of **Gabrielle**.

Gabrielle feminine form of Gabriel; diminutive forms are **Gabbie, Gabby**.

Gaea the Latin form of **Gaia**.

Gaia earth, in Greek mythology the goddess of the earth; the Latin form is **Gaea**.

Gail a diminutive form of **Abigail**, now used independently; variant forms are **Gale, Gayle**.

Galatea white as milk, in Greek mythology a statue brought to life (*Greek*).

Gale a variant form of **Gail**.

Galia wave (*Hebrew*).

Gardenia the name of a flowering plant with fragrant flowers, called after Dr Alexander Garden, used as a first name (*New Latin*).

Garland the name for a wreath or crown of flowers used as a first name (*Old French*).

Garnet the name of a deep-red gemstone used as a first name (*Old French*).

Gay the quality of being joyous used as a first name; also used as a boy's name.

Gayle a variant form of **Gail**.

Gaynor a medieval English form of **Guinevere**.

Gazella like a gazelle or antelope (*Latin*).

Gemma a gem (*Italian*); a variant form is **Jemma**.

Geneva a variant form of **Genevieve**; the name of a Swiss city, used as a first name.

Genevieve meaning uncertain, possibly tribe woman (*Celtic*).

Geneviève the French form of **Genevieve**.

Georgia, Georgiana, Georgina forms of George; a diminutive form is **Georgie**.

Geraldine feminine form of Gerald.

Germaine feminine form of Germain; a variant form is **Jermaine**.
Gerrie, Gerry diminutive forms of **Geraldine**.
Gertrude spear maiden (*Germanic*); diminutive forms are **Gert, Gertie, Trudi, Trudy**.
Ghislaine (*French*).
Gigi a French diminutive form of **Georgine, Virginie**.
Gilberta, Gilberte forms of Gilbert; diminutive forms are **Gill, Gillie, Gilly**.
Gilda sacrifice (*Germanic*).
Gill a diminutive form of **Gilberta, Gilberte, Gillian**.
Gillian feminine form of Julian; diminutive forms are **Gill, Gillie, Gilly**.
Gillie a diminutive form of **Gilberta, Gilberte, Gillian**.
Gilly a diminutive form of **Gilberta, Gilberte, Gillian**.
Gina a diminutive form of **Georgina**, also used independently.
Ginnie, Ginny a diminutive form of **Virginia**.
Giovanna the Italian form of **Jane**.
Gipsy a variant form of **Gypsy**.
Gisela the Italian and Spanish forms of **Giselle**.
Gisèle the French form of **Giselle**.
Giselle promise, pledge (*Germanic*).
Gitana gipsy (*Spanish*).
Gladys the anglicized Welsh form of **Claudia**.
Gleda Old English version of Gladys.
Glenda clean and good (*Welsh*); a variant form is **Glenys**.
Glenna feminine form of Glen.
Glenys a variant form of **Glenda**; a variant form is **Glynis**.
Gloria glory (*Latin*).
Glynis form of **Glyn**; a variant form of **Glenys**.
Godiva gift of God (*Old English*).
Golda, Golde gold (*Yiddish*).
Goldie an anglized form of **Golda**; fair-haired (*Old English*).
Grace graceful one (*Latin*); a diminutive form is **Gracie**.
Gráinne loved (*Irish Gaelic*); a variant form is **Grania**.

Grania a variant form of **Gráinne**.

Greer form of the surname **Grier**.

Greta a diminutive form of **Margaret**.

Gretchen a diminutive form of **Margaret, Margarete**.

Grete a diminutive form of **Margarete**.

Griselda, Grizelda stone heroine (*Germanic*); diminutive forms are **Grissel, Grizel**.

Guida guide (*Old English*).

Guinevere white and soft; the name of the wife of King Arthur (*Celtic*).

Gussie, Gusta diminutive forms of **Augusta**.

Gwenda a diminutive form of **Gwendolen**, used independently.

Gwendolen, Gwendolin, Gwendolyn white ring or bow (*Welsh*); diminutive forms are **Gwen, Gwenda, Gwennie**.

Gwyneth blessed (*Welsh*).

Gypsy the name for a member of a people who live a nomadic life, used as a first name; a variant form is **Gipsy**.

Hagar flight (*Hebrew*).

Haidee modest, honoured (*Greek*); a variant form of **Heidi**.

Halcyon, Halcyone variant forms of **Alcyone**.

Hannah grace (*Hebrew*); a variant form is **Ann**; a diminutive form is **Nana**.

Happy an English adjective, meaning feeling, showing or expressing joy, now used as a first name (*Old English*).

Haralda feminine form of Harold.

Harmony the word for the

quality of concord used as a first name (*Greek*).

Harriet, Harriot feminine forms of Harry; diminutive forms are **Hattie, Hatty**.

Hattie, Hatty a diminutive form of **Harriet**.

Hayley a surname, meaning hay clearing, used as a first name (*Old English*); a variant form is **Haley**.

Hazel the name of a tree used as a first name (*Old English*).

Heather the name of a purple or white-flowered plant of the heath family used as a first name (*Old English*).

Hebe young (*Greek*). In Greek mythology, the daughter of Zeus and goddess of youth and spring.

Hedda war, strife (*Germanic*); a variant form is **Heidi**.

Heidi a variant form of **Hedda**, now used independently; a variant form is **Haidee**.

Helen, Helena light (*Greek*); diminutive forms are **Nell, Lena**.

Helene the German form of **Helen**.

Hélène the French form of **Helen**.

Helga healthy, happy, holy (*Old Norse*).

Helma protection (*Germanic*).

Héloïse a French variant form of **Éloise**.

Henrietta feminine form of Henry; diminutive forms are **Hettie, Hetty, Netta, Nettie**.

Henriette the French form of **Henrietta**.

Hephzibah my delight is in her (*Hebrew*); a diminutive form is **Hepsy**.

Hera queen of heaven; in Greek mythology, the sister and wife of Zeus (*Greek*). Her counterpart in Roman mythology is Juno.

Hermione a name derived from that of Hermes.

Hermosa beautiful (*Spanish*).

Herta of the earth (*Old English*); a variant form is **Hertha**.

Hertha a variant form of **Herta**.

Hester, Hesther variant forms of **Esther**.

Hettie, Hetty diminutive forms of **Henrietta**.

Heulwen sunshine (*Welsh*).

Hibernia the Latin name for

Ireland used as a first name.

Hibiscus marsh mallow, the name of a brightly flowering plant used as a first name (*Greek/Latin*).

Hilary, Hillary cheerful; merry (*Latin*).

Hilda battle maid (*Germanic*); a variant form is **Hylda**.

Holly, Hollie the name of the red-berried tree used as a first name (*English*).

Honey the word for a sweet substance used as a term of endearment and as a first name.

Honor, Honora variant forms of **Honour**.

Honoria honourable (*Latin*); diminutive forms are **Nora, Norah, Noreen**.

Honour the word for personal intregity used as a first name; variant forms are **Honor, Honora**.

Hope the word for the feeling of expectation used as a first name (*English*).

Horatia feminine form of Horace.

Hortensia, Hortense of the garden (*Latin*).

Huberta feminine form of Hubert.

Hyacinth the name of the flower adapted from the name of the hero of Greek mythology whose blood, after his killing by Apollo, caused a flower to spring up.

Hylda a variant form of **Hilda**.

Hypatia highest (*Greek*).

Ianthe violet flower (*Greek*).

Ibby a diminutive form of **Isabel**.

Ida god-like (*Germanic*).

Idabell god-like and fair.

Idonia sufficient (*Latin*).

Idony, Idonie in Norse mythology, the keeper of the

golden apples of youth (*Norse*).

Ignatia feminine form of Ignatius.

Ilona a Hungarian form of **Helen**; a diminutive form is **Ilka**.

Ilse a diminutive form of **Elisabeth**.

Imogen from *innogen*, girl, maiden (*Celtic*), used by Shakespeare for one of his characters in *Cymbeline* and misspelled by him or his printer.

Imperial relating to an emperor (*Latin*).

Ina a diminutive form of names ending in *-ina*, e.g. **Georgina**, **Wilhelmina**.

India the name of the country used as a first name.

Inés, Inez Spanish forms of **Agnes**.

Inga, Inge diminutive forms of **Ingrid**.

Inger a variant form of **Ingrid**.

Ingrid maiden of Ing, the god of fertility (Frey) (*Old Norse*); a variant form is **Inger**; diminutive forms are **Inga, Inge**.

Innes island (*Scots Gaelic*).

Iola a variant form of **Iole**.

Iolanthe violet flower (*Greek*).

Iole violet (*Greek*); a variant form is **Iola**.

Iona yew tree (*Celtic*), the name of the Scottish Hebridean island used as a first name.

Ione a violet (*Greek*).

Iphigenia strong (*Greek*).

Irene peace (*Greek*); a diminutive form is **Renie**.

Iris rainbow (*Greek*).

Irma noble one (Germanic).

Isa a diminutive form of **Isabel**.

Isabel, Isabella Spanish forms of **Elizabeth**, now used as separate English-language names; variant forms are **Isobel**, **Ishbel** (particularly in Scotland); diminutive forms are **Ibby, Isa, Izzie, Izzy, Tib, Tibbie**.

Isabelle the French form of **Isabel**.

Isadora a variant form of **Isidora**.

Iseabail, Ishbel Scots forms of **Isabel**.

Iseult a French and Welsh form of **Isolde**.

Ishbel a variant form of **Isabel**.

Isidora feminine form of Isidore; a variant form is **Isadora**.

Isla, Islay a Scottish island name used as a first name.

Isobel a variant form of **Isabel**.

Isola isolated, alone (*Latin*).

Isolde, Isolda, Isold beautiful aspect (*Welsh*).

Ita, Ite thirst (for truth) (*Irish Gaelic*).

Ivana feminine form of Ivan.

Ivy the name of the plant used as a first name (*Old English*).

Izzie, Izzy diminutive forms of **Isabel**.

Jacinta the Spanish form of **Hyacinth**.

Jacinth a variant form of **Hyacinth**.

Jackie a diminutive form of **Jacqueline**, used independently.

Jacqueline a feminine form of Jacques; a variant form is **Jaqueline**; diminutive forms are **Jackie, Jacqui** (*French*).

Jacquetta feminine form of James.

Jade the name of the light-green semi-precious stone used as a first name.

Jael wild she-goat (*Hebrew*).

Jancis a combination of **Jan** and **Frances**; a diminutive form is **Jan**.

Jane form of **John**; variant forms are **Janet, Janeta, Janette, Janice, Janine, Jayne, Jean, Joan**; diminutive forms are **Jan, Janey, Janie**.

Janet, Janeta, Janette variant forms of **Jane**; a diminutive form is **Jan**.

Janice a variant form of **Jane**.

Janine a variant form of **Janey**.

Jaqueline a variant form of **Jacqueline**; a diminutive form is **Jaqui**.

Jasmine, Jasmin the name of the flower used as a first name; variant forms are **Jessamine, Jessamyn, Yasmin, Yasmine**.

Jayne a variant form of **Jane**.

Jean a variant form of **Jane**; a diminutive form is **Jeanie**.

Jeanette, Jeannette a diminutive form of **Jeanne**, now used independently as an English-language name.

Jeanne the French form of **Jane**; a diminutive form is **Jeanette**.

Jehuda feminine form of Jehudi; a variant form is **Yehuda**.

Jemima, Jemimah dove (*Hebrew*); diminutive forms are **Mima, Mina**.

Jemma a variant form of **Gemma**.

Jenna, Jenni, Jennie diminutive forms of **Jane, Jennifer**, now used independently; a variant form is **Jenny**.

Jennifer, Jenifer the Cornish form of **Guinevere**; diminutive forms are **Jen, Jennie, Jenny**.

Jenny a diminutive form of **Jennifer**, now used independently; a variant form is **Jennie**.

Jeremia feminine form of Jeremiah.

Jermaine a variant form of **Germaine**.

Jerusha possessed; married (*Hebrew*).

Jess a diminutive form of **Jessica, Jessie**.

Jessamine, Jessamyn variant forms of **Jasmine**.

Jessica God is looking (*Hebrew*); a diminutive form is **Jess**.

Jessie, Jessy diminutive forms of **Janet**, now used as names in their own right.

Jewel the name for a precious stone or valuable ornament used as a first name.

Jezebel domination (*Hebrew*).

Jill a diminutive form of **Gillian, Jillian**, now used independently.

Jillian feminine form of Julian; diminutive forms are **Jill, Jilly**.

Joan, Joann, Joanna, Joanne feminine forms of John; diminutive forms are **Joanie, Joni**.

Jocelyn, Jocelin, little Goth (*Germanic*); diminutive forms are **Jos, Joss**.

Jodie, Jody diminutive forms of **Judith**, now used independently.

Johanna the Latin and German form of **Jane**.

Joni a diminutive form of **Joan**.

Jordana feminine form of Jordan.

Josceline variant form of **Jocelyn**.

Josephine feminine form of Joseph; diminutive forms are **Jo, Josie, Phenie**.

Josette a French diminutive form of **Josephine**, now used independently.

Josie a diminutive form of **Josephine**.

Joy the name of the feeling of intense happiness used as a first name (*English*).

Joyce sportive (*Latin*).

Juana the Spanish form of **Jane**; a diminutive form is **Juanita**.

Judie, Judi diminutive forms of **Judith**, now used independently.

Judith of Judah (*Hebrew*); diminutive forms are **Jodie, Judy**.

Judy a diminutive form of **Judith**, now used independently.

Julia feminine form of Julius; a variant form is **Juliana**; a diminutive form is **Julie**.

Juliana a variant form of **Julia**.

Julie, Juliet diminutive forms of **Julia**, now used independently.

Julienne feminine form of Julien.

Julieta a Spanish form of **Julia**.

Juliette the French form of **Julia**, now used as an English-language form.

June the name of the month used as a first name (*Latin*).

Juno queen of heaven, in Roman mythology the equivalent of **Hera** (*Latin*).

Justina, Justine feminine forms of Justin.

Kalantha, Kalanthe variant forms of **Calantha**.

Kalypso a variant form of **Calypso**.

Kara a variant form of **Cara**.

Karen a Dutch and Scandinavian form of **Katherine**.

Karin a Scandinavian form of **Katherine**.

Kate a diminutive form of **Katherine**, also used independently.

Katerina a variant form of **Katherine**.

Kath, Kathie, Kathy diminutive forms of **Katherine**.

Katharina, Katharine German forms of **Katherine**; a diminutive form is **Katrine**.

Katherine pure (*Greek*); diminutive forms are **Kate, Kath, Katie, Katy, Kay, Kit, Kittie**.

Kathleen an Irish form of **Katherine**.

Kathryn an American form of **Katherine**.

Katie a diminutive form of **Katherine**, now used independently.

Katrine a diminutive form of **Katharina**; a variant form of **Katriona**; the name of a Scottish loch, meaning wood of Eriu, used as a first name.

Katriona a variant form of **Catriona**; a variant form is **Katrine**.

Katy a diminutive form of **Katherine**, now used independently.

Kayla, Kayleigh, Kayley derivation uncertain, possibly slender (*Irish Gaelic*), a combination of **Kay** and **Leigh**, or a variant form of **Kelly**.

Keely beautiful (*Gaelic*).

Keira a variant spelling of **Ciara**.

Kelly a surname, meaning descendant of war, frequently

used as a first name (*Irish Gaelic*).

Kerry the name of the Irish county used as a first name.

Keturah incense (*Hebrew*).

Kezia, Keziah the cassia tree (*Hebrew*); diminutive forms are **Kizzie, Kizzy**.

Kim a diminutive form of **Kimberley**, used independently.

Kimberley a surname, meaning wood clearing, frequently used as a first name (*Old English*); a diminutive form is **Kim**.

Kirstel a German form of **Christine**.

Kirsten a Scandinavian form of **Christine**.

Kirstie, Kirsty a diminutive form of **Kirstin**, used independently.

Kirstin a Scots form of **Christine**; a diminutive form is **Kirstie.**

Kittie, Kitty diminutive forms of **Katherine**.

Kizzie, Kizzy diminutive forms of **Kezia**.

Kora a variant form of **Cora**.

Kristeen a variant form of **Christine**.

Kristina the Swedish form of **Christina**.

Kylie a combination of Kyle and **Kelly**.

Kyna wisdom (*Gaelic*).

Kyrena a variant form of **Cyrena**.

Lacey a surname, meaning from Lassy in the Calvados region of Normandy, sometimes used as a first name (*Old French*).

Laetitia happiness (*Latin*); variant forms are **Latisha, Letitia**.

Lala tulip (*Slavic*).

Lalage chattering (*Greek/*

Latin); a diminutive form is **Lallie, Lally**.

Lana a variant form of **Alana**.

Lara a diminutive form of **Larissa** (*Latin*).

Laraine a variant form of **Lorraine**; the queen (*Old French*).

Larissa, Larisa meaning uncertain, possibly happy as a lark (*Greek/Russian*); diminutive forms are **Lara, Lissa**.

Latisha a variant form of **Laetitia**.

Laura laurel, bay tree (*Latin*); a diminutive form is **Laurie**.

Laurabel a combination of **Laura** and **Mabel**.

Laurel a name for the evergreen bay tree, used as a first name.

Lauren feminine form of Laurence; a variant form is **Loren**; a diminutive form is **Laurie**.

Lavender the English name of the plant that bears blue or mauve flowers, used as a first name.

Laverne the alder tree (*Old French*); diminutive forms are **Verna, Verne**.

Lavinia, Lavina of Latium in Italy (*Latin*).

Lea a variant form of **Leah, Lee**.

Leah languid, or wild cow (*Hebrew*); variant forms are **Lea, Lee**.

Leane a variant form of **Leanne, Liane**.

Leanne a combination of **Lee** and **Anne**; a variant form is **Leane**.

Leanora, Leanore German variant forms of **Eleanor**.

Leda mother of beauty; in Greek mythology, a queen of Sparta who was visited by Zeus (who appeared to her in the form of a swan) and gave birth to Helen (*Greek*).

Lela a variant form of **Leila**.

Lena a diminutive form of **Helena**, etc., also used independently.

Lenora a variant form of **Leonora**.

Leona a variant form of **Leonie**.

Leonarda feminine form of Leonard.

Leonie feminine form of Leo, Leon; a variant form is **Leona**.

Leonora an Italian form of **Eleanor**; a variant form is **Lenora**; a diminutive form is **Nora**.

Lesley feminine form of Leslie.

Leticia, Letitia variant forms of **Laetitia**.

Letha forgetfulness (*Greek*).

Lettice a variant form of **Laetitia**; diminutive forms are **Lettie**, **Letty**.

Lexie, Lexy diminutive forms of **Alexandra**.

Liana, Liane, Lianna, Lianne sun (*Greek*); variant forms are **Leane, Leana, Leanna**.

Libby a diminutive form of **Elizabeth**.

Lidia an Italian and Spanish form of **Lydia**.

Liese a diminutive form of **Elisabeth**, now used independently.

Lil a diminutive form of **Lilian, Lily**.

Lila a variant form of **Leila**; a diminutive form of **Delilah**.

Lilac bluish (*Persian*), the English name of the syringa plant with fragrant purple or white flowers, used as a first name.

Lilah a variant form of **Leila**; a diminutive form of **Delilah**.

Lili a variant form of **Lilie**.

Lilian a diminutive form of **Elizabeth**; a diminutive form is **Lily;** a variant form is **Lillian**.

Lilias, Lillias Scottish forms of **Lilian**.

Lilibet a diminutive form of **Elizabeth**.

Lilie a German form of **Lily**; a variant form is **Lili**.

Lilith of the night (*Hebrew*).

Lilli a variant form of **Lily**.

Lillian a variant form of **Lilian**.

Lily the name of the flowering plant with showy blossoms used as a first name; a variant form is **Lilli**; a diminutive form is **Lil**.

Lin a diminutive form of **Linda**.

Lina a diminutive form of **Selina** and names ending in -lina, -line.

Linda a diminutive form of **Belinda, Rosalind**, etc., now used independently; a variant form is **Lynda**; diminutive forms are **Lin, Lindie, Lindy**.

Lindie a diminutive form of **Linda**.

Lindsay, Lindsey a surname, meaning island of Lincoln, frequently used as a first name; variant forms are **Linsay, Linsey, Linzi, Lynsay, Lynsey**.

Lindy a diminutive form of **Linda**.

Linnette a variant form of **Lynette**.

Linsay, Linsey variant forms of **Lindsay**.

Linzi a variant form of **Lindsay**.

Lis a diminutive form of **Elisabeth**.

Lisa a diminutive form of **Elizabeth**, now used independently; a variant form is **Liza**.

Lisbeth a diminutive form of **Elisabeth**.

Lisette a diminutive form of **Louise**.

Lissa a diminutive form of **Larissa, Melissa**.

Livia a variant form of **Olivia**.

Liz a diminutive form of **Elizabeth**.

Liza a variant form of **Lisa**.

Lizbeth a diminutive form of **Elizabeth**.

Lizzie, Lizzy diminutive forms of **Elizabeth**.

Lois meaning uncertain, possibly good, desirable (*Greek*).

Lola a diminutive form of **Dolores, Carlotta**, now used independently.

Lona a diminutive form of **Maelona**.

Lorelei the name of a rock in the River Rhine from where, in German legend, a siren lured boatmen, used as a first name.

Loren a variant form of **Lauren**.

Loretta a variant form of **Lauretta**.

Lorna a name invented by R. D. Blackmore, possibly from Lorne, for the heroine of his novel *Lorna Doone*.

Lorraine a surname meaning man from Lorraine (bold and famous) used as a first name (*Old French*); a variant form is **Laraine**.

Lottie, Lotty diminutive forms of **Charlotte**.

Louella a combination of **Louise** and **Ella**.

Louisa feminine form of Louis; a diminutive form is **Lulu**.

Louise the French form of **Louisa**, now used widely as an English-language form; diminutive forms are **Lisette, Lou**.

Luce a diminutive form of **Lucy**.

Lucia feminine form of Lucian.

Lucienne feminine form of Lucien.

Lucilla a diminutive form of **Lucia**.

Lucille, Lucile French forms of **Lucia**, now used as English-language forms.

Lucinda a variant form of **Lucia**; a diminutive form is **Cindy**.

Lucrèce a French form of **Lucretia**.

Lucretia, Lucrece from lucrum, gain (*Latin*).

Lucrezia an Italian form of **Lucretia**.

Lucy a popular form of **Lucia**; a diminutive form is **Luce**.

Luella a variant form of **Louella**.

Luise the German form of **Louisa**; a diminutive form is **Lulu**.

Lulu a diminutive form of **Louisa**.

Lydia of Lydia in Asia Minor (*Greek*).

Lyn a diminutive form of **Lynette, Lynsay**.

Lynda a variant form of **Linda**; diminutive forms are **Lyn, Lynn, Lynne**.

Lynette an English form of **Eluned**; variant forms are **Lynnette, Linnette**.

Lynn pool or waterfall (*Celtic*); also a diminutive form of **Lynda**; a variant form is **Lynne**.

Lynnette a variant form of **Lynette**.

Lynsay, Lynsey variant forms of **Lindsay**.

Lyris she who plays the harp (*Greek*).

Lysandra feminine form of Lysander.

Mabel a diminutive form of **Amabel**, also used independently; a variant form is **Maybelle**.

Maddie, Maddy diminutive forms of **Madeleine**.

Madeleine, Madeline from Magdala on the Sea of Galilee (*French*); a variant form is **Magdalene**; diminutive forms are **Maddie, Maddy, Mala**.

Madge diminutive forms of **Margaret, Marjory**.

Madonna my lady, a title of the Virgin Mary (*Italian*).

Mae a variant form of **May**.

Maelona princess (*Welsh*); a diminutive form is **Lona**.

Maeve intoxicating (*Celtic*); variant forms are **Mave, Meave**.

Magda a German and Scandinavian form of **Magdalene**.

Magdalene, Magdalen variant forms of **Madeleine**.

Maggie diminutive forms of **Margaret**.

Magnolia the name of a tree with showy flowers, named after the French botanist Pierre Magnol, used as a first name.

Mahalia tenderness (*Hebrew*).

Mai, Mair Welsh forms of **May**.

Maida the name of a place in Calabria in Spain, where a battle was fought in 1806, used as a first name; a diminutive form is **Maidie**.

Mairead an Irish form of **Margaret**.

Mairi Scots Gaelic form of **Mary**.

Maisie diminutive forms of **Margaret**, also used independently.

Mala a diminutive form of **Madeleine**.

Malvina smooth brow (*Scots Gaelic*).

Manda a diminutive form of **Amanda**.

Mandy diminutive form of

Amanda, Miranda, now used independently.
Manuela God with us (*Spanish*).
Marcella feminine form of Marcellus.
Marcia feminine form of Marcius; a variant form is **Marsha**; diminutive forms are **Marcie, Marcy**.
Mared a Welsh form of **Margaret**.
Margaret a pearl (*Greek*); diminutive forms are **Greta, Madge, Maggie, Margie, May, Meg, Meggie, Meta, Peg**.
Margarete the Danish and German form of **Margaret**; diminutive forms are **Grete, Gretchen**.
Margarita the Spanish form of **Margaret**; a diminutive form is **Rita**.
Margaux a variant form of **Margot**.
Margery in the Middle Ages a diminutive form of **Margaret**, but now a name in its own right; a variant form is **Marjorie**; a diminutive form is **Madge, Marge**.
Margherita the Italian form of **Margaret**; a diminutive form is **Rita**.
Margie diminutive form of **Margaret**.
Margo, Margot diminutive forms of **Margaret, Marguerite**, now used independently; a variant form is **Margaux**.
Marguerite the French form of **Margaret**; diminutive forms are **Margo, Margot**.
Mari an Irish and Welsh form of **Mary**.
Maria the Latin, Italian, German, and Spanish forms of **Mary**; a diminutive form is **Ria**.
Marianne a French and German form of **Marion**; a compound of **Mary** and **Ann**
Maribella a compound of **Mary** and **Bella**.
Marie a French form of **Mary**; a diminutive form is **Marion**.
Marietta diminutive form of **Maria**, also used independently
Marigold the name of the golden flower used as a first name.
Marilyn diminutive form of

Mary, also used independently.

Marina of the sea (*Latin*).

Marion a variant form of **Mary**.

Marisa summit (*Hebrew*).

Marjorie, Marjory variant forms of **Margery**.

Marlene a contraction of **Maria Magdalena** (*German*).

Marsha a variant form of **Marcia**.

Marta the Italian, Spanish and Swedish form of **Martha**, now used as an English-language form; a variant form is **Martita**.

Martha lady (*Hebrew*); diminutive forms are **Mat, Mattie**.

Marti a diminutive form of **Martina, Martine**.

Martina forms of **Martin**; a diminutive form is **Marti**.

Martine the French form of **Martina**, now used as an English-language form; a diminutive form is **Marti**.

Martita a variant form of **Marta**; a diminutive form is **Tita**.

Mary bitter; their rebellion; star of the sea (*Hebrew*); variant forms are **Marion, Miriam**; diminutive forms are **Mamie, May, Minnie, Mollie, Polly**.

Maryann, Maryanne compounds of **Mary** and **Ann** or **Anne**.

Marylou a compound of **Mary** and **Louise**.

Mathilda a variant form of **Matilda**.

Mathilde the French form of **Matilda**.

Matilda mighty war (*Germanic*); a variant form is **Mathilda**; diminutive forms are **Mat, Mattie, Tilda, Tilly**.

Mattie a diminutive form of **Matilda**.

Maud, Maude a medieval form of **Matilda**.

Maura an Irish form of **Mary**.

Maureen an Irish diminutive form of **Mary**.

Mave a variant form of **Maeve**; a diminutive form of **Mavis**.

Mavis an alternative name of the song thrush used as a first name (*English*); a diminutive form is **Mave**.

Maxine feminine form of Max.

May diminutive form of

Margaret, Mary; the name of the month used as a first name; a variant form is **Mae**; a diminutive form is **Minnie**.

Maybelle a compound of May and Belle; a variant form of **Mabel**.

Meave a variant form of **Maeve**.

Medea meditative; in Greek mythology the princess who helped Jason obtain the Golden Fleece from her father (*Greek*).

Meg, Meggie diminutive forms of **Margaret**.

Megan Welsh form of **Meg**, now used independently.

Meironwen white dairymaid (*Welsh*).

Melanie black (*Greek*).

Melinda honey (*Greek*) plus the suffix -inda.

Melisande the French form of **Millicent**.

Melissa a bee (*Greek*); a diminutive form is **Lissa**.

Melody a word for tune or tunefulness, used as a first name.

Mercedes the Spanish form of **Mercy** (as a plural).

Mercy the quality of forgiveness used as a first name (*English*).

Meredith a surname, meaning lord, used as a first name (*Welsh*).

Meri a variant form of **Merry**.

Meriel a Welsh form of **Muriel**; variant forms are **Merle, Meryl**.

Merri, Merrie variant forms of **Merry**.

Merry the adjective, meaning cheerful, mirthful, joyous, used as a first name (*Old English*); a diminutive form of **Meredith**; variant forms are **Meri, Merri, Merrie**.

Meryl a variant form of **Meriel, Merrill**.

Meta a diminutive form of **Margaret**.

Mia a diminutive form of **Maria**.

Michaela feminine form of Michael.

Michèle, Michelle French forms of **Michaela**, now used as English-language forms.

Mignon a word, meaning sweet, dainty, used as a first name (*French*); a diminutive form is **Mignonette**; a diminutive form is **Minette**.

Mil a diminutive form of **Mildred, Millicent**.

Milcah queen (*Hebrew*).

Mildred gentle counsel (*Germanic*); diminutive forms are **Mil, Millie**.

Millicent work and strength (*Germanic*); a diminutive form is **Millie**.

Millie diminutive form of **Amelia, Emilia, Mildred, Millicent**.

Mima a diminutive form of **Jemima**.

Mimi an Italian diminutive form of **Maria**.

Mimosa the English name of a tropical shrub with yellow flowers used as a first name; from the Latin word for imitative.

Minerva wise one; in Roman mythology the counterpart of Athena, the goddess of wisdom.

Minette a diminutive form of **Mignonette**.

Minna, Minne love (*Germanic*); diminutive forms of **Wilhelmina**.

Minnie a diminutive form of **Mary, May, Wilhelmina**.

Minta a diminutive form of **Araminta**.

Mira a diminutive form of **Mirabel, Miranda**.

Mirabel, Mirabelle wonderful (*Latin*); diminutive forms are **Mira, Myra**.

Miranda wonderful (*Latin*); diminutive forms are **Mira, Myra**.

Miriam variant form of **Mary**.

Mitzi a German diminutive form of **Maria**.

Mo diminutive form of **Maureen**.

Modesty an English word from *modestus* (*Latin*) for the quality of being shy or humble, sometimes used as a first name.

Moira an anglicized Irish form of **Mary**; a variant form is **Moyra**.

Mollie, Molly diminutive forms of **Mary**, now used independently.

Mona noble (*Irish Gaelic*).

Monica of uncertain meaning, but possibly advising (*Latin*).

Monique the French form of

Monica, now also used as an English-language form.
Morag great (*Scots Gaelic*).
Morgana feminine form of Morgan.
Morna a Scots variant form of **Myrna**.
Morven a Scottish placename, meaning sea gap, used as a first name (*Scots Gaelic*).
Moyra a variant form of **Moira**.
Muriel sea bright (*Celtic*).
Myfanwy my fine one (*Welsh*).
Myra a name invented by the poet Fulke Greville, possibly as an anagram of **Mary**, or to mean she who laments (*Greek*); a diminutive form of **Mirabel, Miranda**.
Myrna beloved (*Irish Gaelic*); a variant form is **Morna**.
Myrtle the name of the shrub used as a first name.

Naamah loved (*Hebrew*).
Nadezhda hope (*Russian*).
Nadia an English, French and Italian form of **Nadezhda**.
Nadine a French variant form of **Nadia**.
Naida the water nymph (*Latin*); a variant form is **Naiada**.
Nairne from the river (*Gaelic*).
Nan a diminutive form of **Ann, Nancy, Nanette**.
Nana a diminutive form of **Hannah**.
Nancy a variant form of **Ann**, now used independently; diminutive forms are **Nan, Nina**.
Nanette a variant form of Ann, now used independently; a diminutive form is **Nan**.
Naomi pleasantness (*Hebrew*).
Napea girl of the valley (*Latin*); diminutive forms are **Napaea, Napia**.
Nara nearest and dearest (*English*).

Narda fragrant perfume. The lingering essence (*Latin*).
Natalie a French form of **Natalya** now used as an English-language form.
Natalya Christmas (*Latin/Russian*).
Natasha a Russian diminutive form of **Natalya**.
Nathania gift of God (*Hebrew*); diminutive forms are **Natene, Nathene, Nathane**.
Neale feminine form of Neil.
Nell, Nellie, Nelly diminutive forms of **Eleanor, Ellen, Helen**.
Nerice, Nerima, Nerine, Nerissa from the sea (*Greek*).
Nerys lord (*Welsh*).
Nessa a diminutive form of **Agnes, Vanessa**.
Nessie a diminutive form of **Agnes**.
Nesta a Welsh diminutive form of **Agnes**.
Netta, Nettie diminutive forms of **Henrietta**.
Niamh bright (*Irish Gaelic*).
Nicole feminine form of Nicholas; variant forms are **Nicola, Nicolette, Colette**; diminutive forms are **Nicky, Nikkie**.
Nikki a diminutive form of **Nicole**.
Nina a diminutive form of **Nancy**.
Ninette (*French*) a variant form of **Ann**.
Ninon a variant form of **Ann** (*French*).
Nita a diminutive form of **Anita, Juanita**.
Nixie water sprite (*Germanic*); diminutive forms are **Nissie, Nissy**.
Noël, Noel Christmas (*French*).
Nola famous (*Irish Gaelic*).
Nona ninth (*Latin*).
Nora, Norah a diminutive form of **Eleanor, Honora, Leonora**, also used independently.
Noreen an Irish form of **Nora**.
Norma a rule (*Latin*), but probably invented as the name of the heroine of Bellini's opera.
Nuala a diminutive form of **Fionnuala**, also used independently.

Octavia feminine form of Octavius.

Octavie a French form of **Octavia**.

Odelia, Odelie variant forms of **Odile**.

Odette homely (*Germanic*).

Odile, Odille rich, wealthy (*Germanic*); variant forms are **Odelia, Odelie, Ottilie, Otilie**.

Ofra a variant form of **Ophrah**.

Olga the Russian form of **Helga**.

Olive an olive (*Latin*); a variant form is **Olivia**.

Olivia a variant form of **Olive**; a diminutive form is **Livia**.

Olwen white track (*Welsh*).

Olympia heavenly (*Greek*).

Ona a diminutive form of names ending *-ona*, e.g. Fiona.

Oona, Oonagh variant forms of **Una**.

Opal the name of the iridescent gemstone used as a first name, precious stone (*Sanskrit*).

Ophelia help (*Greek*).

Ophrah, Ophra fawn (*Hebrew*); variant forms are **Ofra, Oprah**.

Oprah a modern variant of **Ophrah**.

Oriana, Oriane golden (*Latin*).

Oriel strife (*Germanic*).

Orla golden girl (*Irish Gaelic*).

Orlanda feminine form of Orlando.

Orna feminine form of Oran.

Ottilie, Otilie variant forms of **Odile**.

Ozora strength of God (*Hebrew*).

Paige, Page a surname, meaning page, used as a first name (*Old French*).

Paloma the Spanish word for dove used as a first name.

Pamela a name invented by th · poet Sir Philip Sidney derived from the Greek work for honey; a diminutive form is **Pam**.

Pandora gifted (*Greek*); in Greek mythology, the first woman on earth.

Pansy thought (*French*); the name of the garden flower used as a first name.

Paola the Italian form of **Paula**.

Patience patience (*Latin*).

Patricia feminine form of Patrick; diminutive forms are **Paddy, Pat, Patsy, Pattie, Patty, Tricia**.

Patsy a diminutive form of **Patricia**.

Pattie, Patty diminutive forms of **Martha, Patience, Patricia**.

Paula feminine form of Paul.

Paulette a French form of **Paula**.

Paulina, Pauline feminine forms of Paul.

Peace the word for the condition of tranquillity or calm used as a first name (*Latin*).

Pearl the name of the lustrous white gem used as a first name.

Peg, Peggie, Peggy diminutive forms of **Margaret**.

Penelope wave (*Greek*); diminutive forms are **Pen, Penny**.

Penny diminutive form of **Penelope**, now used independently.

Peony healing (*Greek*), the name of a plant with pink, red, white or yellow flowers used as a first name.

Perdita lost one (*Latin*), used

by Shakespeare as a first name for a character in *The Winter's Tale*.

Peronel a contraction of **Petronel**.

Persephone of uncertain meaning; in Greek mythology, goddess of the underworld (*Greek*).

Persis a Persian woman (*Greek*).

Petra feminine form of Peter.

Petrina a variant form of **Petra**.

Petronel, Petronella feminine form of Petronius, a Roman family name (*Latin*).

Petula asking (*Latin*); a diminutive form is **Pet**.

Petunia the name of a plant with white, blue or purple flowers used as a first name.

Phebe a variant form of **Phoebe**.

Phedra bright (*Greek*).

Phèdre the French form of **Phedra**.

Phemie, Phamie diminutive forms of **Euphemia**.

Phenie a diminutive form of **Josephine**.

Philippa feminine form of Philip; diminutive forms are **Phil, Pippa**.

Philomena love and strength (*Greek*).

Phoebe moon (*Greek*); a variant form is **Phebe**.

Phyllida a variant form of **Phyllis**.

Phyllis a green bough (*Greek*).

Pia from the Latin word meaning pious.

Pilar pillar (*Spanish*), an allusion to the Virgin Mary who appeared to St James the Greater, standing on a pillar.

Pippa a diminutive form of **Philippa**.

Polly diminutive form of **Mary**, now used independently.

Pollyanna a compound of **Polly** and **Anna**.

Pomona fruitful (*Latin*).

Poppy the name of the plant that has a bright red flower used as a first name.

Portia gift (*Latin*).

Prima feminine form of Primo.

Primrose the name of the yellow spring flower used as a first name.

Priscilla from *prisca*, ancient

(*Latin*); diminutive forms are **Cilla, Prissie**.

Prudence the abstract noun for the quality of caution or circumspection, used as a first name (*Latin*); diminutive forms are **Prue, Prudie**.

Prue a diminutive form of **Prudence, Prunella**.

Prunella plum (*Latin*); a diminutive form is **Prue**.

Psyche of the soul (*Greek*).

Queenie a diminutive form of the word queen, the supreme woman, used as a first name (*Old English*).

Quenby a surname, meaning queen's manor, used as a first name (*Old English*).

Querida beloved, a Spanish term of endearment used as a first name.

Quinta feminine form of Quinto; a variant form is **Quintina** (*Latin*).

Rachel lamb (*Hebrew*); a variant form is **Rachelle**; diminutive forms are **Rae, Ray**.

Rachele the Italian form of **Rachel**.

Rachelle a variant form of **Rachel**.

Rae a diminutive form of **Rachel**.

Raisa tolerant (*Greek*).

Ramona wise *(Spanish)*.
Ranee, Rani queen *(Hindi)*.
Raphaela feminine form of Raphael.
Raquel the Spanish form of **Rachel**.
Raven the name of a bird, used as a first name *(Old English)*.
Rayne a surname, meaning mighty army, used as a first name; a variant form is **Raine**.
Rea a variant form of **Rhea**.
Rebecca, Rebekah the Hebrew word means noose and the name has come to mean bound, faithful; diminutive forms are **Beckie, Becky**.
Regina queen *(Latin)*.
Reine queen *(French)*.
Renata a diminutive form of **Renée**.
Renée feminine form of René.
Reva feminine form of Reeve.
Rexanne a compound of Rex and **Anne**; a variant form of **Roxanne**.
Rhea, Rheia of uncertain origin and meaning; in Roman mythology she was the mother of Remus and Romulus; in Greek mythology she was the mother of several gods, including Zeus; a variant form is **Rea**.
Rhiain maiden *(Welsh)*.
Rhiannon goddess *(Welsh)*.
Rhoda rose *(Greek)*.
Rhona a variant form of **Rona**.
Ria a German diminutive form of **Maria**.
Rica a diminutive form of **Roderica**.
Rina a diminutive form of names ending *-rina*.
Rita a diminutive form of **Margarita, Margherita**, used independently.
Roberta feminine form of Robert.
Robina feminine form of Robin.
Rochelle little rock *(French)*.
Roderica feminine form of Roderick; a variant form is **Rodericka**; a diminutive form is **Rica**.
Rohanna feminine form of Rohan.
Róisín, Roisin an Irish form of **Rose**.
Rolanda, Rolande feminine forms of Roland.

Roma a Roman (*Latin*).

Romy a diminutive form of **Rosemary**.

Rona the name of a Scottish island, meaning rough rocky island, used as a first name (*Old Norse*); a variant form is **Rhona**.

Ronalda feminine form of Ronald; diminutive forms are **Ronnie, Ronny**.

Rosa a rose (*Latin*); diminutive forms are **Rosetta, Rosie**.

Rosabel, Rosabella, Rosabelle a compound of **Rosa** and **Bella**.

Rosalie, Rosalia little and blooming rose.

Rosalind, Rosaline beautiful as a rose (*Latin*); a diminutive form is **Linda**.

Rosamund, Rosamond horse protection; famous protection (*Germanic*); rose of the world (*Latin*).

Rosanne, Rosanna compounds of **Rose** and **Anne**; variant forms are **Roseanne, Roseanna**.

Rose the English form of **Rosa**; the name of the flower used as a first name; diminutive forms are **Rosette, Rosie**.

Roseanne, Roseanna variant forms of **Rosanne, Rosanna**.

Rosemarie a combination of **Rose** and **Marie**.

Rosemary the name of the plant associated with remembrance used as a first name; diminutive forms are **Romy, Rosie**.

Rosetta a diminutive form of **Rosa**.

Rosette a diminutive form of **Rose**.

Rosie a diminutive form of **Rosa, Rose, Rosemary**, now also used independently.

Rowena fame and joy (*Germanic*).

Roxanne, Roxane dawn of day (*Persian*); a variant form is **Rexanne**; a diminutive form is **Roxie**.

Ruby the name of the red gemstone used as a first name.

Ruth friend (*Hebrew*).

Sabina Sabine woman (*Latin*).
Sabine a French and German form of **Sabina**.
Sabra restful (*Hebrew*).
Sabrina of uncertain meaning, linked to the name of the River Severn (*pre-Celtic*), or princess (*Latin*); a variant form is **Zabrina**.
Sadie a diminutive form of **Sara**.
Sal a diminutive form of **Sally, Sarah**.
Salina from the salty place (*Greek*).
Sally, Sallie diminutive forms of **Sara**, now used independently.
Sacha help (*Greek*); a variant form is **Sasha**.
Salome peaceful (*Hebrew*).
Salvia sage (*Latin*).
Samantha listener (*Aramaic*); or a compound of **Sam** and **Anthea**; a diminutive form is **Sam**.
Samuela feminine form of Samuel.
Sandie a diminutive form of **Alexandra**.
Sandra a diminutive form of **Alessandra, Alexandra**, now used independently.
Sapphire from *saphir*, beautiful (*Hebrew*); the name of the blue precious stone used as a first name.
Sarah, Sara princess (*Hebrew*); diminutive forms are **Sadie, Sal, Sally**.
Sasha a variant form of **Sacha**.
Savanna a form of the word for an open grassland used as a first name (*Spanish*).
Scarlett a variation of the word scarlet, a bright red colour, used as a first name by Margaret Mitchell in her novel *Gone with the Wind*.
Selina, Selena parsley; heavenly (*Greek*); a diminutive form is **Lina**.

Selma feminine form of Anselm.

Semele single (*Latin*).

Senga slender (*Gaelic*); backward spelling of **Agnes**.

Seonaid a Gaelic form of **Janet**.

Septima feminine form of Septimus.

Seraphina, Serafina of the seraphim, of burning faith (*Hebrew*).

Serena calm; peaceful (*Latin*).

Shannon the name of the Irish river, meaning the old one, used as a first name.

Shari a diminutive form of **Sharon**.

Sharon a Biblical placename mentioned in the Song of Solomon, used as a first name (*Hebrew*); a diminutive form is **Shari**.

Sheelagh a variant form of **Sheila**.

Sheelah petition (*Hebrew*); a variant form of **Sheila**.

Sheena an anglicized form of **Sine**.

Sheila, Shelagh anglicized forms of **Sile**; variant forms are **Sheelagh, Sheelah**.

Shelley a surname, meaning clearing on a bank, frequently used as a first name (*Old English*).

Sheree, Sheri variant forms of **Chérie**.

Sheryl a variant form of **Cheryl**.

Shirley a surname and placename, meaning thin clearing, used as a first name; a diminutive form is **Shirl**.

Shona the anglicized form of **Seonaid**.

Sian the Welsh form of **Jane**.

Sibeal an Irish form of **Sybyl**.

Sibyl, Sibylla soothsayer (Greek); variant forms are **Sybyl, Sybylla**; a diminutive form is **Sib**.

Sidney a surname, meaning wide island, used as a first name; a variant form is **Sydney**; a diminutive form is **Sid**; also used as a boy's name.

Sidonia, Sidonie, Sydony of Sidon (*Latin*).

Sierra the name for a mountain range, used as a first name (*Spanish*).

Sigrid fair and victorious (*Old*

Norse); a diminutive form is **Siri**.

Sile the Gaelic form of **Celia, Cecily**, often rendered in English as **Sheila, Shelagh**, etc.

Silvia of a wood (*Latin*); a variant form is **Sylvia**.

Silvie the French form of **Silvia**.

Simona feminine form of Simon; a diminutive form is **Sim**.

Simone the French form of **Simona**.

Sine a Gaelic form of **Jane**, often rendered in English as **Sheena**.

Sinead an Irish Gaelic form of **Janet**.

Siobhan an Irish Gaelic form of **Jane**.

Sioned a Welsh form of **Janet**.

Sisley a variant form of **Cecily**; diminutive forms are **Sis, Sissie, Sissy**.

Sofie the French form of **Sophie**.

Solveig house strong (*Old Norse*).

Sonya, Sonia a Russian diminutive form of **Sophia**.

Sophia wisdom (*Greek*).

Sophie, Sophy diminutive forms of **Sophia**, now used independently.

Sophronia of a sound mind (*Greek*).

Sorcha bright one (*Irish Gaelic*).

Spring desire (*Sanskrit*), the name of the season between winter and summer used as a first name.

Stacy, Stacey, Stacie diminutive forms of **Eustacia, Anastasia**, now used independently.

Star, Starr an English form of **Stella**.

Stasia a diminutive form of **Anastasia**.

Steffi, Steffie diminutive forms of **Stephanie**.

Stella star (*Latin*).

Stephanie feminine form of Stephen; diminutive forms are **Steffi, Steffie**.

Storm the word for a meteorological condition of violent winds and rain, hail or snow used as a first name (*Old English*).

Sukey, Sukie diminutive forms of **Susan**.

Summer season (*Sanskrit*); the name of the season, used as a personal name.

Susan the English form of **Susanna**; diminutive forms are **Sue, Sukey, Sukie, Susie, Susy**.

Susanna, Susannah lily (*Hebrew*); a variant form is **Suzanna**.

Susanne a German form of **Susanna**.

Suzanna a variant form of **Susanna**.

Suzanne a French and German form of **Susan**.

Sybille the French form of **Sybyl**.

Sybyl, Sybilla variant forms of **Sibyl, Sibylla**; a diminutive form is **Syb**.

Sylvia a variant form of **Silvia**.

Sylvie the French form of **Silvia**.

Tabitha gazelle (*Aramaic*); diminutive forms are **Tab, Tabby**.

Talitha maiden (*Aramaic*).

Tallulah a placename, meaning spring water, used as a first name (*North American Indian*).

Tamar palm tree (*Hebrew*); diminutive forms are **Tammie, Tammy**.

Tamara the Russian form of **Tamar**.

Tammie, Tammy diminutive forms of **Tamar, Tamsin**, sometimes used independently.

Tamsin a Cornish contraction of **Thomasina**, now used independently; diminutive forms are **Tammie, Tammy**.

Tania, Tanya diminutive forms of **Tatiana, Titania**, now used independently.

Tanisha born on Monday (*Hausa*).

Tansy immortal (*Greek*), the name of a medicinal plant bearing yellow flowers, used as a first name.

Tara a placename, meaning rocky assembly place, used as a first name (*Irish Gaelic*).

Tatiana form of a Roman family name of unknown meaning (*Latin*); diminutive forms are **Tania, Tanya**.

Tempest the word for a violent storm used as a first name (*Latin*).

Teresa the Italian and Spanish forms of **Theresa**.

Terese a variant form of **Theresa**.

Teri a diminutive form of **Theresa**.

Terri a diminutive form of **Teresa, Theresa**, now used independently.

Terry a diminutive form of **Teresa**.

Tess, Tessa, Tessie diminutive forms of **Esther, Teresa, Theresa**; now used independently.

Thalia flourishing blossom (*Greek*).

Thea a diminutive form of **Althea, Dorothea**, now used independently.

Thecla god glory (*Greek*).

Theda a diminutive form of **Theodora, Theodosia**.

Thelma a name coined in the 19th century by Marie Corelli for her novel *Thelma*, possibly derived from Greek word for wish.

Theodora feminine form of Theodore; diminutive forms are **Dora, Theo**.

Theodosia gift of God (*Greek*).

Theophila feminine form of Theophilus.

Theresa harvester (*Greek*); diminutive forms are **Teri, Terri, Terry, Tess, Tessa, Tessie, Tracey, Tracie, Tracy**.

Thérèse the French form of **Theresa**.

Thirza pleasantness (*Hebrew*); variant forms are **Thyrza, Tirza**.

Thomasina, Thomasine feminine forms of Thomas.

Thora feminine form of Thor.

Thordis a variant form of **Tordis**.

Thyrza a variant form of **Thirza**.

Tib, Tibbie (*Scots*) diminutive forms of **Isabel, Isabella**.

Tiffany the manifestation of God, the festival of Epiphany (*Greek*).

Tilda, Tilde diminutive forms of **Matilda**.

Tilly a diminutive form of **Matilda**.

Timothea feminine form of Timothy.

Tina a diminutive form of **Christina, Christine**, etc., also used independently.

Tirza, Tirzah variant forms of **Thirza**.

Tita feminine form of Titus; a diminutive form of **Martita**.

Titania giant, in medieval folklore wife of Oberon and queen of fairies (*Greek*); diminutive forms are **Tania, Tanya**.

Tobey feminine form of Toby; a variant form is **Tobi**.

Tomasina, Tomina feminine forms of Thomas.

Toni diminutive forms of **Annette, Antoinette, Antonia**, now used independently.

Tonia a diminutive form of **Antonia**.

Tonie diminutive forms of **Annette, Antoinette, Antonia**, now used independently.

Topaz the name of a white gemstone used as a first name.

Tordis Thor's goddess (*Old Norse*); a variant form is **Thordis**.

Tory a diminutive form of **Victoria**.

Tracie a diminutive form of **Teresa, Theresa**, now used independently.

Tricia a diminutive form of **Patricia**.

Trilby a name coined by George du Maurier in the 19th century for the heroine of his novel *Trilby*.

Trisha a diminutive form of **Patricia**.

Trista sorrowful (*Latin*).

Trix, Trixie diminutive forms of **Beatrice**.

Truda, Trudie, Trudy diminutive forms of **Gertrude**.

Tullia peaceful (*Gaelic*).

Ulrica English form of **Ulrike**.

Ulrike feminine form of Ulrich.

Una a lamb; hunger (*Irish Gaelic*); form of one (*Latin*) used by Edmund Spenser in *The Faerie Queene*.

Unity the abstract noun for the quality of harmony or concord, used as a first name in the Puritan tradition.

Urania heavenly—the name of one of the Muses (*Greek*).

Ursula she-bear (*Latin*).

Ursule the French form of **Ursula**.

Valentina feminine form of Valentine; a diminutive form is **Val**.

Valentine strong (*Latin*); a diminutive form is **Val**; also used as a boy's name.

Valerie strong (*Latin*); a diminutive form is **Val**.

Vanessa a name invented by Jonathan Swift for Esther Vanhomrigh, created from the prefix of her surname plus the suffix *essa,* derived from her christian name; a diminutive form is **Nessa**.

Venetia from Venice (*Latin*).

Vera faith (*Russian*).

Verity truth (*Latin*).

Verne, Verna diminutive forms of **Laverne**.

Verona a variant form of **Veronica**.

Veronica true image (*Latin*); a variant form is **Verona**; diminutive forms are **Ronnie, Ronny**.

Vesta in Roman mythology, the goddess of the hearth (*Latin*).

Vi a diminutive form of **Viola, Violet**.

Vicki, Vickie, Vicky diminutive forms of **Victoria**, now used independently.

Victoria victory (*Latin*); diminutive forms are **Tory, Vickie, Vita**.

Vida beloved (*Hebrew*); a Welsh feminized form of David.

Vincentia feminine form of Vincent.

Viola, Violet a violet (*Latin*); a diminutive form is **Vi**.

Violetta the Italian form of **Viola, Violet**.

Virginia virginal (*Latin*); a diminutive form is **Ginnie**.

Vita a diminutive form of **Victoria**.

Viv a diminutive form of **Vivien**.

Vivien, Vivienne feminine form of Vivian; a diminutive form is **Viv**.

Wanda a variant form of **Wenda**.

Wenda wanderer (*Germanic*); a variant forms are **Wanda, Wendy**.

Wendy a variant form of **Wenda**; popularized by the writer J. M. Barrie who used the name for the leading female a character in his play *Peter Pan*.

Whitney a surname and placename, meaning white island or Witta's island, now used as a first name (*Old English*).

Wilfrida, Wilfreda feminine forms of Wilfrid.

Wilhelmina, Wilhelmine protector (*Germanic*); diminutive forms are **Elma, Minna, Minnie, Wilma**.
Willa diminutive feminine form of Will, William.
Williamina feminine form of William.
Wilma a diminutive form of **Wilhelmina**; feminine form of William.
Winifred joy and peace (*Old English*); diminutive forms are **Freda, Win, Winnie, Wynn, Wynne**.
Wynn, Wynne fair (*Celtic*); a diminutive form of **Winifred**.

Xanthe yellow (*Greek*).
Xaviera feminine form of Xavier.
Xena, Xene, Xenia hospitality (*Greek*).
Yasmin, Yasmine variant forms of **Jasmine**.
Yehuda a variant form of **Jehuda**.
Yolanda, Yolande a variant form of **Viola**.
Yseult an old French form of **Isolde**.
Yvette feminine form of Yves.
Yvonne feminine form of Yves.
Zabrina a variant form of **Sabrina**.
Zara flower (*Arabic*).
Zelma a variant form of **Selma**.
Zenobia having life from Zeus (*Greek*).
Zinnia the name of a plant with brightly coloured flowers used as a first name; named after the German botanist J. G. Zinn.
Zoë, Zoe life (*Greek*).